WILL I EVER PEE ALONE AGAIN?

WILL I EVER PEE ALONE AGAIN?

Emma Conway

sphere

SPHERE

First published in Great Britain in 2020 by Sphere

1 3 5 7 9 10 8 6 4 2

Copyright © Emma Conway 2020

The moral right of the author has been asserted.

A CIP catalogue record for this book
is available from the British Library.

ISBN 978-0-7515-8006-8

Typeset in Minion by M Rules
Printed and bound in Great Britain by
Clays Ltd, Elcograf S.p.A.

Papers used by Sphere are from well-managed forests
and other responsible sources.

Sphere
An imprint of
Little, Brown Book Group
Carmelite House
50 Victoria Embankment
London EC4Y 0DZ

An Hachette UK Company
www.hachette.co.uk

www.littlebrown.co.uk

For Erin and Ethan.
Love you mostest.

Hello!

In 2013 I decided to start a blog. As a tired mum to a baby and a toddler, I began shouting into the black void of the internet hoping someone somewhere would shout back at me. I wanted to feel that the way I looked, the way I parented and the way I felt about my relationship was normal. As it was so very different to the online world that portrayed motherhood as perfect.

This book of poems will hopefully make you go, 'it's not just me!' and is best read hiding in the bathroom with a pack of biscuits and a huge mug of tea. I hope they make you giggle and realise that sometimes being ordinary can be extraordinary.

Emma
@brummymummyof2

Wait

I look at your face
And you look at me
I sniff your soft head
As you bounce on my knee
I hold your chubby fingers
And count your tiny toes
I kiss your rosebud lips
And tap your turned-up nose
You do a little burp
I pretend it was a smile
I really should put you down
But let's sit here for a while.

A Baby Poo Haiku

A poo is brewing
Your little face strains in pain
BOOM! An explosion.

Who is Most Tired?

'*I'm* most tired,' you sadly say.
'No, you're not. Not a chance. No way!
'It's really me who needs to sleep,'
he starts to rock and gently weep.
'I don't believe you. I was up all night.'
'You're so f*cking wrong. It is I who is right.'
You look at each other. So knackered and broken,
arguing over who first was woken.
You have a think. And become inspired
to just yell louder . . . '**I AM MOST TIRED!**'

Mum Crush

There's one thing I always think about when I
      watch kids' TV:
'Do you think that presenter would fancy me?'
I like to think he would, and that he'd sweep me
      off my feet –
In The Night Garden, where we'd first meet.
He would look at my tired face and in a sexy
      voice say,
'You knackered-looking mums really
      make my day.
'When I'm talking about Peppa, I'm thinking
      about you,
'you're in my heart, when I'm singing about poo.'
Daddy Pig shouts 'OINK' and I snap back
      to reality.
I stare at the telly. He stares back at me.

He's dancing around now, but I'm sure he just
    gave me a smile?
That's the most action this mum has seen in a
    while . . .

Parenting-life in Limericks

There was a young woman called Mum,
who always awoke before the sun,
her husband slept in,
she rather hated him,
nightfeeds are really not fun.

There once was a mum who was lucky,
she got sick down her top so was mucky,
she hid it quite well,
no one could tell,
till her toddler announced she was 'YUCKY!'

There was a young man called Dad,
who made his wife incredibly mad,
he didn't hear the baby,
she yelled, 'You're lazy!'
Now he's lying in bed feeling sad.

There once was a dad who was fuming,
about the calories he kept on consuming,
his belly did grow,
his metabolism was slow,
he didn't laugh when his wife said, 'you're
        blooming!'

There was a young woman called Mum,
who declared doing the washing, 'NO FUN!'
she hated to clean,
it made her quite mean,
she'd rather watch MIC on her bum.

Love Is

Love is
your baby pissing in your eye
and you still looking at him with adoration.

I Dream of Soft White Pillows

I dream of soft white pillows
Somewhere I can lay my head
Preferably in a sterile hotel
Alone in a giant bed
No one would shout, 'MUMMY'
I would be happy as can be
I wouldn't have to change nappies
I could drink a hot cup of tea
I would lie in the bath for hours
And chat to all my friends
Put a series on Netflix
And watch it till the end
I'd have a poo in silence
And scroll for hours on my phone
It probably sounds quite selfish
But sometimes I dream that I'm alone.

Unsolicited Advice

I don't need to put my child in mittens
I'm not worried they may be allergic to kittens
they certainly aren't feeling too cold
yes they still have a dummy at 18 months old
please leave me alone with your advice
I know you're just trying to be helpful and nice
but you're making me feel oh so bad
I'm left worrying and emotionally quite sad
I understand that you're just doing what you
    think's right
but I don't care if your kids sleep
    through the night
I'm really trying to do my very best
even though you think I'm a disorganised mess
I'm learning to be a mum and that's really hard

and your unsolicited advice is leaving my
    confidence scarred
so next time you see me, smile and give
    me a cuddle
and say, 'you know what, it's normal to feel all of
    a muddle.'

The Tantrum

The sun is shining
Happiness is all around
It begins
With a rumble
A moan
A look
A welly gets thrown
Somebody shouts, 'what's wrong?'
It's me
A scream
A drop to the floor
Confusion
An elderly lady smiles
'Somebody isn't very happy'
'No I'm not!' I want to answer
The air is filled with sobbing
There is a stamp
I begin to see the problem
It's obvious
The apple has a bruise
I dig out a biscuit
I put on the welly
I dry the tears
We kiss and make up
With an angry cuddle

Soggy biscuit on my mouth
Perfection
Until I say he can't have an ice cream
And the welly goes flying through the air again.

Potty Training

All I want is for you to poo in the potty.
Please just use toilet roll to wipe your botty.

Just do a wee. You'll get a chocolate bar!
For god's sake don't take a sh*t in Nanny's car.

In the shopping centre you start to shout,
'I NEED TO POO POO, I HAVE TO LET IT OUT!'

You pull down your trousers as you start to crap.
Other mums look on sadly. I just want to nap.

But then one day, you smile and stare up at me,
I look inside your red potty and I spy a wee.

I phone up your Daddy and we start to cheer –
a pile of piss is the highlight of our year.

What's That Smell?

What's that smell?
It gave me a start.
Is it a poo?
Or is it a shart?
It's hanging about
Jesus, what a stink
I worry what other mothers
In soft play will think
I try to grab you
To sniff your bum
But you just laugh at me
Then scream, 'RUUNNN'
Someone makes a sick noise
And looks right at me
Another says, 'Good God!
'It's putting me off my tea.'
I finally grab you
And your bum smells fresh!
But I notice sh*t on my leggings
Oh, the shame! I'm the mess.

Tipsy Mum

Pre-babies I'd go out and drink lots and
    lots and lots.
Blue WKD, white wine and many tequila shots.
I'd dance around with my mates feeling
    soooo sexy.
But now at home you'll find me, with a lukewarm
    cup of tea.

Occasionally I make it out and have a glass of fizz.
I shove a bit of make-up on and really
    look the biz.
After half a glass I'm giggling and talking
    really loud.
By glass two I'm dancing in the middle
    of a crowd.

By glass three I'm doing a full routine to my
     queen, Beyoncé.
My friends are cheering me on and everyone
     stares my way.
I decide to get in a taxi when I start to
     feel less fine.
I look at my watch as I get in. It's only half
     past nine.

Naps Save Lives

Date night!
All alone at last.
I look at you.
You look at me.
We look at each other.
We look at the bed.
In unison, in hushed,
provocative tones we say . . .
'Shall we just have a nap?'

Snot

There once was a toddler who was cranky
His mum wiped his nose with a hanky
He let out a shout
More snot shot out
She dropped the tissue and said, 'God
     you're manky!'

Seasons Haikus

Spring has so much rain
Stop fighting with the brolly
You will hurt someone.

Summer is so hot
Stand still for suntan lotion
Or you will get burnt.

Autumn is so wet
Please stop jumping in puddles
Your socks will get soaked.

Winter is so cold
Please put your hat and gloves on
This is relentless.

The Crap Wife

Sometimes I wonder what you think of me
As I serve fish fingers again for tea
You walk in from work and I look broken
In my dressing gown like I've just been woken
With milk on my top
And sick in my hair
If you look closely
You'll see poo somewhere
Sometimes I cry and call your phone
Not to say, 'I love you'
But more just to moan
Before we had kids we had sex all the time
Now if I show a tit a toddler shouts 'MINE'
We put them to bed and we look at each other
Suddenly your wife again and not just
      their mother.

Ode to Friday Night

Oh Friday night, you wondrous thing.
The best day of the week, you make my heart
     sing.
I get home from work and off comes my bra,
my boobs touch my knees, they hang
     down that far,
my pyjamas go on and my slippers do too,
I've been thinking of this moment since a
     quarter to two.
I start to plan what to eat around a half past five,
I can't remember a day when I've felt so alive.
We put the kids to bed, there's a knock
     at the door,
'Is it the Chinese?' (We couldn't be sure.)
'IT IS! IT IS!' we scream and we shout –
the happiest people who are not going out.

Staying in is the best thing in life.
Ignoring your husband. Ignoring your wife.
On opposite couches, just you and me:
full up on prawn crackers, in silent harmony.

Loneliness

It's strange to feel so lonely.
When you're never alone.
Small hands grabbing at your hair.
Tiny voices calling your name.
Confined to a room full of toys.
Or in a park with strangers you recognize.
But you only know each other as 'Mum'.
A TV blares out but there's nothing for you to see.
You're reading another book aloud but it's not for
      your eyes.

But then a chubby arm goes around your neck,
a sloppy kiss is left on your cheek,
and for a brief moment in time,
you're not alone,
you're right where you are meant to be.

Dirty Mummy Secrets

Sometimes I pretend I don't hear the baby so my
    husband has to get up in the night
Sometimes I eat cold leftovers standing by the sink
Sometimes I use baby wipes to clean the kitchen
Sometimes I use baby wipes to clean my privates
Sometimes I put my pyjamas on at 3pm
Sometimes I don't get dressed
Sometimes I eat chocolate on the toilet to hide
    from the kids
Sometimes I pretend the TV is broken as I can't
    face Peppa again
Sometimes I only shave my ankles if I'm wearing leggings
Sometimes I say 'oh lovely' when I'm not sure
    what my child has said
(Sometimes I use the word 'Sometimes' when I
    mean 'A Lot Of The Time')

Socks

There's washing in the basket
(it never bloody ends)
but there's one thing always missing
and that is our sock friends.
They are meant to come in pairs
yet they always end up alone –
it's as if they really hate me
and want to leave this home.
I sometimes sit and wonder
about an alternate reality,
where a monster sits and eats spare socks
whilst watching the TV.
Perhaps tiny house mice
sleep in them at night,
or maybe they are housing
our resident garden sprite.

It's more likely that I've lost them
but it's a complete mystery to me.
I wish they grew on branches
on a spare sock magic tree.

Before I had Kids

Before I had kids my tits were great,
I'd go afternoon shopping with my best mate.

Before I had kids I'd sleep till noon,
There weren't plastic crap toys covering my
    front room.

Before I had kids I would drink all night,
Spend hours getting ready ensuring my make-up
    was just right.

Before I had kids I watched loads of TV,
I read books in silence over hot coffee.

Before I had kids, I'd wear heels to my job,
Now my hair's cut into a sensible 'mum bob'.

Before I had kids, I wasn't tired all the time,
I didn't have to remove lipstick from a
            toddler screaming, 'MINE!'

But now I have kids, and it's different you see –
I have someone who solely relies on me.

    I can often be seen walking around
                like a mess,
    but then I also have two humans
                declaring I'm 'the best!'

            I miss the lie-ins, the heels and it
                        being just me,
            long leisurely baths, luxuriously
                        drinking hot tea.

But would I want to change a thing? Why,
            of course not!
My children are the most wonderful
            gifts I've got.

Will I Ever Pee Alone Again?

Please stop staring at me whilst I'm on the loo –
I simply want a peaceful poo.
Stop chatting to me whilst I'm having a wee,
and when I wipe my bum – don't climb on my knee.

I lock the door but you bang it down,
you bring toys into the bathroom and I
     start to frown.
My bum hits the seat and you scream,
     'MUMMMMYYYY!'
How do you know I'm hiding in the loo to try to
     drink my tea?

You'll look back when you're a teenager and
     start to cringe
when you realise just how often you saw my minge.

I get jealous when your Dad does an hour-long poo,
as he gets to do it away from you.
You don't care when he goes for a bloody long crap –
but you jump on my head if I dare take a nap.

I know it's because you love me so much,
you need to be able to see my face and such,
you love hearing my voice and making me laugh,
and you like to go to the loo and stare at me when
        I'm in the bath.

One day I'll get to poo alone once more,
without one of you leaning against the door,
I'll be able to scroll through my phone or read a book,
or have five minutes' peace and think, 'thank fook'.

But for now I'll content myself by stopping to think –
when I need to pull myself back from the brink –
that when you're a teen you'll forget to lock the door;
I'll walk straight into the bathroom doing some
        boring mum chore.
You'll scream, 'Get out!' and I'll walk off and laugh
and think of you crapping whilst looking at me
        with my boobs out in the bath.

Fickle

Oh no. 'Big Tommy' is coming to play
I better put all my favourite toys away.
Mummy thinks we should be best mates:
'Please play nicely today. His mum is great!'
There is a knock. He barges through the door,
he grabs three biscuits then shouts, 'MORE!'
Our mums start to laugh over a cup of tea.
He looks like he's six but he's actually three.
Why must they insist we always play?
I want him to get his wellies and GO AWAY!
All of a sudden Tommy's mummy starts to stand,
I see something shiny, glistening in her hand,
'We got you a present. Tommy picked it for you!'
It's a bag of tricks including a plastic poo.
I look at Tommy. We stare at each other . . .
. . . I totally love him and I wish he was my brother.

Mum Friends

I'm here if you ever need to moan
over WhatsApp, text or on the phone.
In the past we would have chatted over wine,
now it's more likely, 'fancy a cuppa at mine?'
It might be months till I see your face
(and then it's a playdate round my place).
We don't dance and get drunk any more
(but we moan about our other halves as if it's the law).
But I need you more now than I needed you then:
my companion in Motherhood and my
        best friend.
Because you send pick-me-up gifs when my
        kids are sick
and always agree when I say my husband's a d*ck.

Holidays are Meant to be Fun

Holidays are meant to be fun
(for everyone else it seems, just not for mum).
We're expected to book it and we have to pack –
apparently giving birth gives us the knack.

We have to remember each and every
        bloody thing:
pants, wellies, buckets, spades and a unicorn-
        shaped rubber ring.
When we finally get to where we are meant to be
someone shouts, 'who forgot to pack toothpaste?'

Oh f*ck that was me!

'I CAN'T REMEMBER EVERYTHING,' I wail
        and I shout.

The family look at each other whilst I start to
        freak out.
'Why do I always have to do it all?' I sob
        with despair.
'I packed pyjamas, cereal and bobbles for hair!'

'Because Mummy, you know you really are
        the best!'
'We wouldn't know what to do! Our packing
        would be a mess!'
I nod my head slowly and sadly agree:
no one can pack for a week in a caravan as
        well as me.

Hairy Legs

From October till May you are always there,
covering me from head to toe like a grizzly bear.
You keep me warm and it feels so right,
even when you poke out of a thick black tight.
My children touch my legs and start to scream:
'ARGH MONSTERS' THIGHS!' God,
      kids are mean.
My husband has gone past the point of caring,
he barely notices the pants I'm wearing.
But as you grow older, it begins to show –
your hair starts at your chin and
      includes your toe.
I've been known to pull out a thick back whisker,
I'm starting to turn into Grotbag's sister.
But I'm happy and content just to be
a cuddly, slightly unsightly, animal-like me.
It will soon be May and I'll despair –
as then I'll have to shave off all my hair.
(Or wear leggings.)

Soft Play

Soft play is grim
Soft play is gross
Full of rotten plastic balls
And soggy cheap toast
My kids love it
And it's evident for all to see
I'll go f*cking ANYWHERE
For a peaceful cup of tea.

Tomorrow I'll Be Better

Tomorrow I'll be better
I promise I won't shout so much.
I promise to sit and read and smile
and not always be in a rush.

Tomorrow I'll be better,
and not tired beyond belief,
and when you ask to watch Peppa Pig again
I won't lie on my bed and weep.

Tomorrow I'll be better,
our lunch will be amazing!
It won't consist of a ham roll, banana
and another pack of raisins.

Tomorrow I'll be better
and I won't snap at Dad,
I won't moan about the washing up,
and I promise I won't look sad.

Tomorrow I'll be better,
I am going to give it a try,
and when you're naughty I'll just roll my eyes
and not shout so much I cry.

Tomorrow I'll be better
because you mean the world to me,
I will forget about the silly rules
and give you ice cream for your tea.

Tomorrow I'll be better,
and hug you till you squeal
and sniff your lovely tiny heads
and threaten to eat you for every meal.

Tomorrow I'll be better.
And if I'm not perfect? That's okay.
I'm trying to do the best I can ...
and tomorrow's just another day.

Mummy Thinks We Hate Each Other

Mummy thinks we hate each other,
but I'm really quite fond of my baby brother.

We sometimes have a cuddle when she can't see
(I definitely know he looks up to me).

But it's far more fun to scrap and fight,
to kick up a fuss when we go to bed at night.

One day we'll be open about how much we care –
until then we'll wind Mum up so she pulls out her hair.

Toilet Roll: A Haiku

One brown cardboard roll
Who will take it down the stairs?
Mum again of course.

Don't Tell Mummy

Don't tell Mummy,
she doesn't need to know.
Just try some chocolate
and go with the flow.
It doesn't really matter
that you've not had your dinner;
it will be our secret.
We're onto a winner!
Don't you worry, Mummy won't get mad.
I'm her free babysitter and also her Dad.

Starting School

I can't believe you're leaving me.
I watch you walk away.
A lump forms in my dry throat.
I've been dreading this very day.
My heart is totally breaking,
I want to yelp, 'DON'T GO!'

I feel abandoned and a little lost inside.
My chest feels like it's torn open wide.
You completely broke my heart.
It's plain for all to see.
But I hide it well, with a big grin,
and wave back as you wave at me.

Sick

Oh no! You've been sick everywhere!
It's on your cuddly toys and in your blonde hair.
Your daddy starts to panic,
your brother starts to shout,
'URGH MUMMY, IT KEEPS ON
        COMING OUT!'
I catch it in my hands and try to keep calm,
I use my 'nice mum' voice to raise no alarm.
'IT STINKS,' someone says.
I give them a look.
They've clearly not read the 'Sick Kid Book'.
I'm joking of course: there is no book.
If you're looking for advice, you're clear out of luck.
So here are some tips for you,
not just about sick but also poo:
try not to gag or scream out loud,
instead give them a cuddle and tell them
        you're proud
that they got it in the sick bowl and not
        on the rug,
and try not to cringe when you give them a hug.
Because when they are ill they just want you –
which sadly may include being smeared in
        their poo.

The School Run

It happens every first day of term.
'I'm going to be better!' But I never learn.
I promise to remember your PE kit,
and that my cakes at the school fair will be a hit.
I'll never go to school and look a mess,
your homework projects will be the best,
I'll note down every fancy dress day –
order an outfit from Amazon? Me? NO WAY!

I'm gonna be the best school-run-mum –
just you wait and see –
you'll be honoured to be my daughter.
Oh so proud of me.

The second day of term
and things start to slide
I've forgotten an important form,
from your form tutor I hide.
I didn't brush my hair
and I forgot to clean my teeth.
I'm wearing yesterday's jumper
with nothing underneath.
But we are here on time!
It's a miracle to see.
(Not gonna lie,
that probably won't happen on day three.)

Tummy

I have a funny relationship with my tummy.
It's soft and squishy and held humans that made
    me a mummy.
I sometimes wish I was a little bit slimmer
(maybe I should stop eating cake then I'd be on to
    a winner).
Sometimes my children say, 'but Mummy it's
    SO wobbly' –
the skin is rippled and stretched and bobbly.
When I run, it goes one way, my boobs the other.
But rather than stopping at one biscuit, I think,
    'sod it, I'll have another.'
I've accepted the fact I'll never be slim.
When I find a top that hides my tum I see
    that as a win.
I like tights that cover it and go right up to my tit.

And a giant pant that goes over it is
        considered a hit.
My belly is just one part of me and doesn't
        represent who I am,
it doesn't stop me from having fun and didn't stop
        me from finding a man.
When I laugh it moves and it's glorious to see
that my kids love my belly, as my belly's
        part of me.
So next time when you see your tum and it makes
        you feel kinda sad,
you can't get into jeans you want and it leaves you
        feeling mad,
focus on the best parts of you: your eyes, your
        nose, your chin.
If you start to love yourself more I'll consider
        this a win!
Your body's just a vessel that holds your
        inside bits,
so ignore your giant belly and your long old
        saggy tits.
Focus on what makes you happy and ignore that
        massive tum,
Never, ever, EVER let it stop you from having
        loads of fun.

If I Only had an Hour

If I only had an hour there is SO much
     I would do,
I would sit undisturbed on the toilet, read *Heat*
     magazine and do a massive poo.
60 minutes is all I need to make me really happy –
not think about tantrums, lack of sleep, or
     changing another sh*tty nappy.
In one hour I could nip upstairs for a lie down,
     and have a little sleep
Instead of breaking down in my messy living
     room and having a little weep.
I would run around the room shouting 'bollocks!'
     And light a million candles,
or jump in bed and check out Kim Kardashian by
     her Twitter handle.
I could skip to the nearest coffee shop and stuff
     my gob with a treat,
and not give two f*cks about what my small
     people have to eat.
In an hour I could have the most amazing bath,
with Lush bath bombs and a book that
     makes me laugh.
60 minutes would give me time to watch my
     favourite *Real Housewives* show

See them swear, shag and slut drop and make me
      wish I was a ho
I suppose I could have sexy time with my other
      half in bed
(but I would much rather eat a Mars Bar and
      watch *Made in Chelsea* instead).
In an hour I could drink copious amounts
      of hot tea,
online shop, read magazines and most
      importantly feel like 'me'.
So if you are looking for a present for a new mum
      that you know,
give them the gift of time to help them not
      feel so low;
whilst they love their kids so very, very much,
      they need a little rest,
to ease their frazzled mind so that they can be
      their best.

Hero

Not all superheroes wear capes
Some take the bins out
Get the suitcases out of the loft
Change a tricky lightbulb
Catch a spider the size of my head
Hold me when I cry
Love me when I'm angry
And instead of fighting crime
They fight with twisted-up Christmas lights.
I don't have to shine a huge bat signal
Just send a worried face emoji
Or a crying cat gif
And they are there, right away
To help me live to see another day.

Night Out

'Let's plan a night out!'
I WhatsApp to say.
'Well I can't do Thursdays.'
'I can't do May.'
'Saturdays are tricky as Kemi has to swim.'
'Can anyone do Fridays?'
I ask on a whim.
'October is looking empty!'
We're currently in March.
I'm never organising fun again:
it's turned into a farce.
We agree to meet in autumn,
on the second Saturday.
I add it to the family diary.
Oh f*ck – we're away.

Mama Bear

'Charlie called me smelly today and he made me cry.'
WHY WOULD CHARLIE DO THAT? (BUT WHY WOULD HE LIE?)
I WANT TO GO TO THE SCHOOL AND PUNCH CHARLIE
        IN THE FACE
I WANT TO GO ROUND HIS HOUSE AND SMASH
        UP THE PLACE
MY BEAUTIFUL CHILD SMELLS OF HEAVEN
        AND THE SUN
TOMORROW I PLAN TO SQUARE UP
        TO HIS MUM

I stop overthinking it and calmly say,
'You'll be best friends in the morning, as it's
        another day.'

Period: A Haiku

That time of the month
You want to kill your husband
Run away, man, run!

Just Smile

Just smile for the photo
I'll settle for a smirk
please, for the camera
God, this is hard work.

I want a lovely piccy
to send to your nan
to share with my friends on WhatsApp
so they think we're a happy clan.

They won't know that I cried
and bribed you with lots of sweets
as we posed in Christmas jumpers
on some super festive streets.

They will say 'what a perfect family
'in their jumpers that do match
'Emma's husband's gorgeous
'such a handsome catch.'

So when you see a social media picture
that's as pretty as can be
I bet you £100
they are like any other family.

Instagram's a snapshot
it doesn't tell the facts
bet those kids are naughty
and act like your kid acts.

Stripes For Life!

There comes a time
in every mum's life
when you realise
all your tops are striped
black, green and red ones
you have blue ones too
you joke with your mates
about forming a Striped Top Crew.

Proud

You always make me so very proud
When you crapped in a potty I cheered aloud
You once played a sheep in the nativity
I couldn't believe you were made by me
I see you in sports day coming in last
I cheer and don't care that you don't run fast
You read me a story and I stare in glee
I gasp when you know the answer to 2×3
It doesn't matter if you don't come in first
If the painting you did in school is the worst
So long as you try your hardest that's all I request
You're my no 1, my champion, always the best.

Stupid Shouty Mum

I hate it when stupid shouty Mum is about
I cringe when I start to hear her shout
Her voice just drones on and on
'PICK UP YOUR COAT, PUT YOUR
      SHOES ON!'
She repeats herself time and time again
She must be so lonely –
Who would want to be her friend?
I bet she cries guiltily into her cold cup of tea.
(I actually know she does. Stupid shouty Mum is me.)

Clock Changes

If I was Prime Minister
the first law I'd pass
is to keep the bloody clock changes
far in the past.

The clocks go forward
your routine goes bad;
bedtime is at seven
and your kids go mad.

'I'M NOT TIRED,'
they shout and scream.
'Yes you are, it's seven,
'What do you mean?!'

They are clever little buggers
as they know it's really six,
and no amount of begging
will this issue fix.

The next day at five
they run into your bed,
they shout, 'GET UP!'
as they jump on your head.

Kids' TV's not started
and you start to stress.
No wonder this bloody country
is in such a mess.

Then the clocks go back
and the kids are again confused
they go to bed at seven
but it's really eight so they're bemused.

So if I could sit in parliament
I'd say, 'Keep the time the same!'
I know the mornings would be dark
which would be bit of a shame . . .

... But my kids would be happy
and I would get some bloody sleep
and the nation's parents
would be ecstatic and not weep.

Father Christmas

It starts in September,
the same every year:
'YOU BETTER BEHAVE
OR SANTA WILL HEAR.'
The next day they're at it again;
having another fight.
'HE'S WATCHING THROUGH THE TELLY.'
They look up and stop with fright.
I sometimes phone him up
and have a little chat.
He's my favourite threat
that man with the red hat.
'YOU WON'T GET ANY PRESENTS!'
'YOU'LL BE ON THAT NAUGHTY LIST!'
They tidy up their rooms,
put down their clenched fists.

HOWEVER, this trick only works well
until Christmas Day –
before he's delivered his presents
and is well on his way.
After December 25th
you're completely on your own.
There's no one to threaten them with;
no pretend saviour on the phone.
I sit and consider my options,
nerves fluttering in my tummy.
But then I have a lightbulb moment:
'THANK F*CK FOR THE EASTER BUNNY!'

My Mummy is the Gruffalo

My mummy has really hairy toes
I've seen strands poking out of her nose
I saw a thick black whisker on her chin
And a curly one behind her shin
I reckon she's the Gruffalo that we read about
She sounds like a monster when she
    starts to shout
My brother doesn't really agree with me
But I think he's just worried she'll eat us for tea.

The Bad Cop

There is always a bad cop.
That bad cop is me:
I make you tidy up your room
and finish veg you had for tea.

Your daddy is the good cop:
he swings you in the air.
He lets you wear what you want
and does not brush your hair.

We come together as a team:
your good cop dad and me.
We keep you grounded and lift you up
and hope you're the happiest you can be.

Parenting Law of Sod

The Parenting Law of Sod
is rather frustrating and odd.
It's like someone is out to get me
Evilly rubbing their hands in pure glee.
When I've looked forward to a night out
    for weeks,
I've put on mascara and blushed up my cheeks,
as I put on my new dress and hoist up a tit,
a child runs in and covers me in sick.
The Parenting Law of Sod lets out a laugh,
as I throw my son and new dress in the bath.
It's as if it hates me having a life;
I should remain at home being a mum and wife.
But I have some breaking news for it!
In my cupboard is a gin load of sh*t! *(hiccup)*
So tonight I'll get drunk alone instead
and plan to still be pissed when I fall into bed.

Today I've Smashed it

It doesn't happen very often.
But when it does it's great.
You relish it so much
you have to text your mate,
'Today was a good day!
'We had so much fun,
'I totally smashed it,
'I rock at being a mum.
'Everyone ate their breakfast,
'No one shouted "YUCK!"
'We got to nursery on time,
'I'm doing great. Thank f*ck!'
Your friend sends a Beyoncé gif
and tells you you're a queen.
This is the proudest
that you have ever been.

You're a Little Bit Different

You're a little bit different
and that's okay you see
as life would be so boring
if you were the same as me.

It's good to enjoy magic
and run around with books
you go dress up as Elsa
ignore the funny looks!

I'll love you whatever
you decide to be
you'll always be my baby boy
the best thing made by me.

Treat everyone with kindness
no matter what their skin
embrace size, shape and gender
because difference is a wonderful thing.

Sometimes it might seem hard
you might not want to be you
but whoever you end up being
I'll love you through and through.

Mum-mobile

A mum had a car that was disgusting
Bashed up doors and a side that was rusting
The floor was a mess
It made her distressed
She often used socks to give it a dusting.

Mother's Day

Mother's Day comes but once a year.
'A day just for us!' you'll hear all mums cheer.
'We love you so much. We see you each day,
'so on Mothering Sunday please go away.
'We want to lie in bed. Gorging on cake,
'we don't want any meals we have to make.
'Please stick those flowers up your bum.
'We just want a day where no one
        screams "MUM!"'

Ikea: A Haiku

'Let's go to Ikea.'
'We won't have a row this time.'
They were wrong of course.

Little Things

I really love my dressing gown
brand-new slippers make my day
when I see a cheeky 3 for 2
I jump and yell 'HOORAY!'

I like to reuse gift bags
and now sigh when I wee
little things make me happy
especially if they're free!

I used to like extravagant items
and probably spent too much
the youth would possibly think
I'm really out of touch.

But as I slide into fresh pyjamas
and put on a brand-new pair of socks
being old and loving simple things
totally bloody rocks!

Home

My home is so messy. It isn't very neat.
Our garden is the most overgrown in the street.
There's a stain on the carpet. We think it's a wee.
I don't know who did it. But I'm certain
    it's not me.
The bath's a bit grubby. There's shoes by the door.
When I put away the washing I start to
    notice more.
There's a thick layer of dust on the living
    room shelf.
Full of books, plastic toys and a hidden
    Christmas elf.
My kids run through the door and flop on
    the couch.
Piling on top of each other until someone
    shouts, 'OUCH!'
I worry they hate the dirt and can't
    stand the mess.
So I ask, 'do you like our house?' They reply, 'IT'S
    THE BEST!'

Bath Time for Mummy

I decide to have a bath –
to have some 'me time' –
full to the brim with bubbles
with a chilled glass of wine.

I step in and relax
and try not to care,
that all around me are bath toys
who silently float by and stare.

They not only judge my body
But also judge my grout
Back off Igglepiggle – I know it's dirty
but you're making me want to get out!

I turn away from Barbie
with her boobs so pert.
I sit on some bloody Lego.
OH MY GOD THAT HURT!

This relaxing bath is beginning
to feel a little bit sh*t,
especially when I wash my hair in shampoo
that's meant to destroy a nit.

So that's my 'me time' over.
I fling a leg over the side
and feel a sadistic satisfaction
as Barbie gets walloped by the tide.

Pamela

You dream of Pamela Anderson
But you've got me instead
There's no supermodel
Lying sexy in your bed
But that doesn't matter
As we have each other . . .
(And some nights I dream
That Gary Barlow is my lover).

Running

Run, run as fast as you can
you can totally catch me
coz I run like your nan.

I struggle to breathe as I speed walk
I can't catch my breath
and can barely talk.

the water pours down, my bottom is wet
who knew that a lady
could produce so much sweat?

my lycra strains to contain my bum
I should have stayed in bed
rather than choosing to run.

but I'm glad I got up
feeling better that I ran
even though other joggers lap me
coz I run like their nan.

Kids' TV

Hooray! Hooray! for kids' TV,
it allows me to have a quiet wee
or push the Hoover hastily around –
I often cheer when I hear the sound
of their favourite inane TV show
as then I know it's GO GO GO!
It's a little bit of time just for me
to have a sneaky cup of tea.
It's very exciting when I get to poo
(during Peppa Pig they don't watch you).
But please don't always rely on TV.
Once or twice it's broken on me.
So always have the tablet to hand,
the best electronic babysitter in this fair land.

Nanny

There once was a nanny called Sandra
To her grandkids' needs she did pander
She gave them some sweets
And big cakes to eat
When told 'you spoil them' she yelled
      'SLANDER!'

Fish Fingers

We're having fish fingers for our tea
I wonder what Nigella would think of me?
But I put that thought right out of my head
when you cheer and smile as I pop them on bread.

You're Doing Amazing, Sweetie

Your friend's just had a baby:
you're as happy as can be.
But I suggest you pop round
to make her a cup of tea –
being a new mum is difficult
it's so hard and oh so tough;
you're supposed to have your sh*t together
but some mothers find it rough.
They may smile to others,
hide their worries deep within,
so it's your job as their mate
to go and see how they've been.
Give them a little cuddle,
take the baby off their hands,
say, 'now go take a shower'
or clean their pots and pans.
Say, 'you look amazing!'
(Even if they look really bad.)
And promise to be only a call away
during times they might be sad.
We were all new mums once
(and some might be again)
so we know how much it's appreciated:
that little bit of help from our friends.

The Row

You've p*ssed me off in front of the kids,
the kitchen sink is full of dirty pans and lids
I want to shout and scream your name
but the children will hear, which is a pain.
I don't want them to know swear words, so you
      are in luck.
But you should know I think you're a stupid ~~fuck~~
'silly, silly Daddy'.

Supermodel Mums

Hey you guys,
Us mums are trendy!
You can forget Chanel,
Gucci or Fendi.
We like wearing stripes of all colours.
And we rock a good stretchy jean.
When we find a legging that fits.
We'll wear them till they split at the seams.
Heels can sod off, Converse works for us.
We need something flat when we run for the bus.
Our coats are giant with a hood that is huge.
Our fleecy pyjamas get our husbands in the mood.
Sunglasses are the best as they cover tired eyes.
Combined with a jazzy scarf to conceal our size.
Tights up to our tits and a flowery frock.
You can keep supermodels as us mums ROCK!

Box Sets Save Lives

Oh box sets, oh box sets
you bring me such joy,
when a new one pops up
I'm like a kid with a new toy.

I have a morbid fascination
with sets about a handsome killer,
and my heart races
over a brand-new horror thriller.

Sitting every night for two weeks
in silence with my other half,
or watching it with utter glee
in a full hot bubble bath.

They mean I don't have to go out
and I can stay in my pit,
I don't have to leave my couch
which for me is a hit!

I can pause it if I need a wee
or to go to get a snack,
watching TV for hours
is better on your back.

When the box set is over
I really am distraught,
but there's no need to panic!
There's one on Amazon we've not bought!

Wet School Runs SUCK

There's always one thing that's guaranteed.
To make me groan and bring me to my knees.
At half past two. Every single weekday.
From the start of September to the
     beginning of May.
I look at the watch and then at the sky.
And wait for a rain drop to fall in my eye.
It's like Mother Nature sits and waits.
She thinks we've not got enough on our plates.
She wants us to wrestle putting feet in
     welly boots.
It's like she thinks kids carrying brollies can be
     classed as a hoot.
'IS THIS FOR REAL?' I scream in despair.
As the rain pours down and flattens my hair.
The kids run out and jump straight in a puddle.

Bags, coats, socks soaking. You're all of a muddle.
You finally arrive home. Your jeggings
     soaked through.
Now Mother Nature played her joke on you.
I'm so sick of doing the wet school run.
I'm wringing wet yet again. Where are you, sun?
I won't hold my breath. And it's plain to see.
You'll always piss it down by a quarter to three.

Days Gone By

My son's just put music on Spotify
it makes me remember days gone by
where I'd sit and wait for my favourite song
paused ready to record by my radio all day long.

I would play outside with my best mate
chat about people from school we hate
go to the corner shop with just 10p
which would buy enough sweets for her and for me.

There was no social media to scroll with
        your thumb
to speak to a boyfriend you had to go via his mum
(after six on their home telephone, your dad
        listening in
no texts or WhatsApping for me and for him).

Filters didn't exist so you could look a mess
with no photographic evidence you barely
        had to stress
life was slower then and our kids will never know
what it feels like to wait a week for their
        favourite TV show.

Everything is instant now, which I think is
        such a shame
they can find an answer just by saying
        Alexa's name
but there's one thing to which we can all admit
being angry at the DJ for speaking over our
        fave pop hit –
a bit at the start and a bit at the end –
so I'm glad Spotify is my kids' best friend.

Kids' Parties are Fun!

 It seems like it's gonna be fun
when you plan a party for your kid
that's one.

They get to two and you start to stress:
their birthday cake needs to be the best.

When they hit three you're on the gin
as they sob over a game they didn't win.

Four and five are a pain in the ass
when you realise you have to invite the
whole class.

Six is stressful at f*cking soft play;
you wish these parties would go away.

It starts to calm down when they
get to seven:
a cinema trip for four seems like heaven.

She's turning eight and wants her friends to stay.
I'm not keen but her dad said, 'okay'.
He says, 'don't worry, it will be great!'
So he's in charge when they stay up late.

The Wave

Oh no. She's waving.
I don't want anyone to see.
I don't want them to know
she's related to me.
She yells, 'I LOVE YOU!'
Squeals, 'HAVE A GOOD DAY!'
I wish she would bore off
and please just walk away.

But when no one is looking
I hug her, then run.
She's loud and annoying.
But I really love my mum.

Growing Older

When you were little you would sing and dance,
you would often be found in the park showing
     your pants,
you would perform for a whole room to a variety
     of tracks,
you would offer unknown children a bite of
     your snacks.

But as you grow older it becomes plain to see:
you get embarrassed being yourself and
     especially of me.
You'll dance in my bedroom and together we
     will laugh,
but you're growing up now and don't need me in
     your bath.

I shout, 'I LOVE YOU SO MUCH,' as you walk
     into school;
you shrug your shoulders like I've broken a rule.
Sometimes you shout, 'IT'S NOT FAIR,' and slam
     the door shut;
I ask you to put your shoes on, you ignore me
     and stay put.

Yet you will forever be my beautiful little girl,
when I think of you you're smiling and doing a
        little twirl.
So whenever you say you want your own space,
you pound the stairs to your room with
        frightening haste,
it's okay, I don't mind, you're allowed to get older,
just know that I'll always be around to offer you
        my shoulder.

Adulting is Crap

I have to go food shopping but I want to
     have a nap.
I must fill the car with petrol. God,
     adulting is crap.
There's a parcel at the post office and bills
     to be paid.
Toilets to be cleaned and bunk beds to be made.
'What to have for dinner?' I think each and
     every night.
I look in the cupboards and give myself a fright.
One can of tuna. Two tins of beans.
I nod my head sadly. As we all know what
     that means.
I have to go food shopping but I want to
     take a nap.
I've still not filled the car up. God,
     adulting is crap.

Guilt: A Haiku

A nagging feeling
Right at the back of your mind
Guilt, motherhood's curse.

Not Quite Beach Ready

'It's time to get beach ready!'
the newspapers start to say.
Oh God. I look in the mirror
and dread to think what I bloody weigh

I try on a new costume;
it won't go over my hips
and no bikini top
can hold in my huge tits

I finally find a costume
that sucks my tummy in,
it contains my giant bottom
as it clings to my pale skin

I buy some brand new flip-flops
and a jazzy bright sarong,
some overpriced sunglasses
even though my budget says it's wrong

I go to the beach nervously
with my family;
what if people stop and stare
and sadly look at me?

My children ask me to run
and frolic in the sea
I say no at first
but give into their plea

I step in the cold water
and shriek as they both cheer
They exclaim 'YOU ARE THE BEST, MUM!'
It really makes my year

No one stares at me
not a second look
I breathe and let my stomach out
and hug my kids ... thank fook.

I Often Watch you Whilst you Sleep

There is something you'll never know.
At night time you put on a show.
Not just for me, but also your dad.
(If you found out you might get mad.)
We creep in and take a peep,
tip toeing to make sure you're asleep,
we stand and wait and look and stare.
You're in a dreamland. You don't know we're there.
We sometimes move your blanket,
or rearrange your teddy,
tidy up your messy room,
get your school uniform ready.
You may be a big girl
but you'll always be our baby.
Will we still watch when you're a teenager?
I can't confirm ... but maybe.

The End

There's one thing I want you to realise:
you, my beauties, are the apples of my eyes.
I know I can be cross and often moan.
Sometimes I struggle to look up from my phone.

But when I think of you, my heart swells in size.
My heart loses a beat when one of you cries.
The smell of you makes me start to swoon.
My eyes light up when you walk in the room.

When I'm old and my hair has turned grey,
When you've both grown up and both
    moved away,
I'll sit on the couch and chat with your dad
about making the best humans the world
    has ever had.

Thank Yous

My first thank you is to anyone who has ever followed me, left a comment, sent a kind DM, or said, 'thank God it's just not just me!' This book of poems is for us. A physical thing we can hold to make us feel that we might not be perfect, but we are doing a great job after all.

This book wouldn't have come into existence without the lovely Emily Barrett from Little, Brown Book Group. Thanks for believing that I could write something and for totally understanding what I wanted it to sound and look like. Thanks to Emanuel Santos for the adorable illustrations and not judging when I emailed to say, 'can you make my boobs a bit bigger please?'

Also huge love to Paul and Grace at Optimus Talent who put up with my wild ideas and who always have my back ... even if sometimes I'm a little bit wrong.

Special mention needs to go to Sarah Turner, who helped guide me through the process of writing this book. Actually scrap that. Who helps guide me just through general every day life. Who knew someone who lived so far away could seem so close via a phone.

I am blessed with an array of amazing mates I couldn't survive without. Always there to make me laugh with a Gary Barlow gif or a daft meme. I know some of you will get a kick out of a namecheck so here goes; Rachael and Dave Atton, Katie Stephens, Sheila O'Neill, Kate Smart, Melissa Webber, Rachel Elford, Sarah Barnes, Jocelyn Reading and The Hillcrest Gang (we survived!). Love you all more than *The Real Housewives* and Fruit Pastilles.

Of course I need to say big thanks to team Wetton. The proudest Mom, Dad and Sister in the whole of Birmingham. Always there to offer advice, an ear when I moan and a way that brings me back to earth with a bump. I'm thankful for the humour of the three of you. And I honestly don't know what I would do without you. Somebody pass Dad a tissue please.

My dearest Erin, you are nine when this book comes out and I'm thankful you made me a mummy. You're smart, you're kind, you're beautiful. I'm so proud of you my heart could pop!

My gorgeous Ethan, you are seven and love me SO hard I can't believe how lucky I am. You're funny, you're creative. I'm happiest when I am sniffing your head and having a cuddle.

Finally, Stephen. You are the calm to my storm. The lead weight to my balloon. You don't bat an eyelid when I say, 'right I'm going to dance in a showgirl outfit – can you film it please?' There is no one in the world I would rather watch TV with and completely ignore on a Friday night.